Journey to Self Love Second Edition

21 Days of Self Love

Master Life Coach Mechelle Canady

Copyright by Mechelle Canady

Published by C-Sharp Publishing Jacksonville, Florida

Formatted Mechelle Canady

Edited by Jolisha Edwards

ISBN: 978-1-7341907-6-2

All Rights Reserved. No part of this publication may be reproduced, stored in a retrieval system, or transmitted in any form or by any means – electronic, mechanical, digital, photocopy, recording, or any order- except for brief quotations in printed reviews, without the prior permission of the writer or publisher

From the Author:

In February of 2019, I wanted to make some changes in my life. I realized that I had failed to love me authentically. I decided I wanted to learn to love me. I also wanted to share my journey to self-love with others in hopes that the changes I have made would encourage others in their journey to self-love. I wanted to change the way I love me and the way I treat me.

Statistically, it takes 21 days to create or break a habit. I wanted to break the habit of self-neglect and create a habit of self-love. For 21 days, I committed to posting a self-love declaration for 21 days on social media. In doing so it was my effort to engage others in their journey. During the 21 days of posting several people said the post helped them and the information would make a terrific book. They felt the information should be shared with the world and from that the writing of this workbook journal began.

I completed the 21 days of posting and in the process, I recommitted to loving me. I am committed to no longer neglecting me. I made several promises to myself throughout the journey to self-love and my desire is by the end of this workbook, you would have done the same. Take the time to do the work so that you can be a better version of you.

In this workbook, you will find 21 self-love lessons to guide you to your desired result of learning you and getting to know the true you.

Each day there is a self-love lesson, a self-love exercise, a self-love journal exercise, and journal pages in the back of the book for you to complete your exercises.

Embrace each day as a new opportunity to change the narrative and LOVE YOU.

About the Author

Hello, my name is Mechelle D. Canady, and I am a Master Certified Life Coach, and Innovator who is driven by an unwavering entrepreneurial spirit. I am an Author, Publisher, Talk Show Host, Blogger, Vlogger, Pod Cast Host and Mentor. My dedication is to helping people become their best versions. I have also earned the reputation in the life coaching sector as "Mrs. GetU2Gether" because of my style of telling the truth in love.

Throughout the past decade or so, I have gained extensive experience in multiple industries, including event planning (since 2004), business consulting (since 2009), and Professional Christian Life Coach (since 2017). Master Life Coach and Certified Trainer (2019) and I have launched Embrace You Training Solutions, a comprehensive training company that focuses on building custom curriculums. Embrace You Coaching is the subsidiary that certifies Life Coaches and Executive Trainers. We have certified over 100 Life coaches since 2019. I published my first book in November 2017 titled Frozen 3A's My Journey to True Forgiveness. Since then, I have also co-authored 3 additional books. Helping others is my passion and now I can help other authors publish their books independently with my new publishing company C-Sharp Publishing.

As a passionate Master Life Coach and Change Agent, I am on a mission to **Impact**, **Impart**, and **Empower** as many people as possible, and create positive change that will continue transforming lives for future generations. I deeply believe that every one of us possesses infinite potential and when we harness that potential, the possibilities are truly endless.

In addition to pursuing my bachelor's degree in Supervision & Management, I currently serve as the Founder & Operator of The Next Chapter 4 Me Consulting Planning & More, the CEO of Coach Mechelle Canady Ministries, Founder of Prissy Printing, the Head Baker of Tyler's Tasty Treats, and the Lead Pastor/Teacher of Embrace You Ministries. Also, the president of Embrace You Outreach Inc and Canady Enterprises.

My heart's desire is to leave a legacy that impacts generations and to create generational wealth to come by being a World Changer.

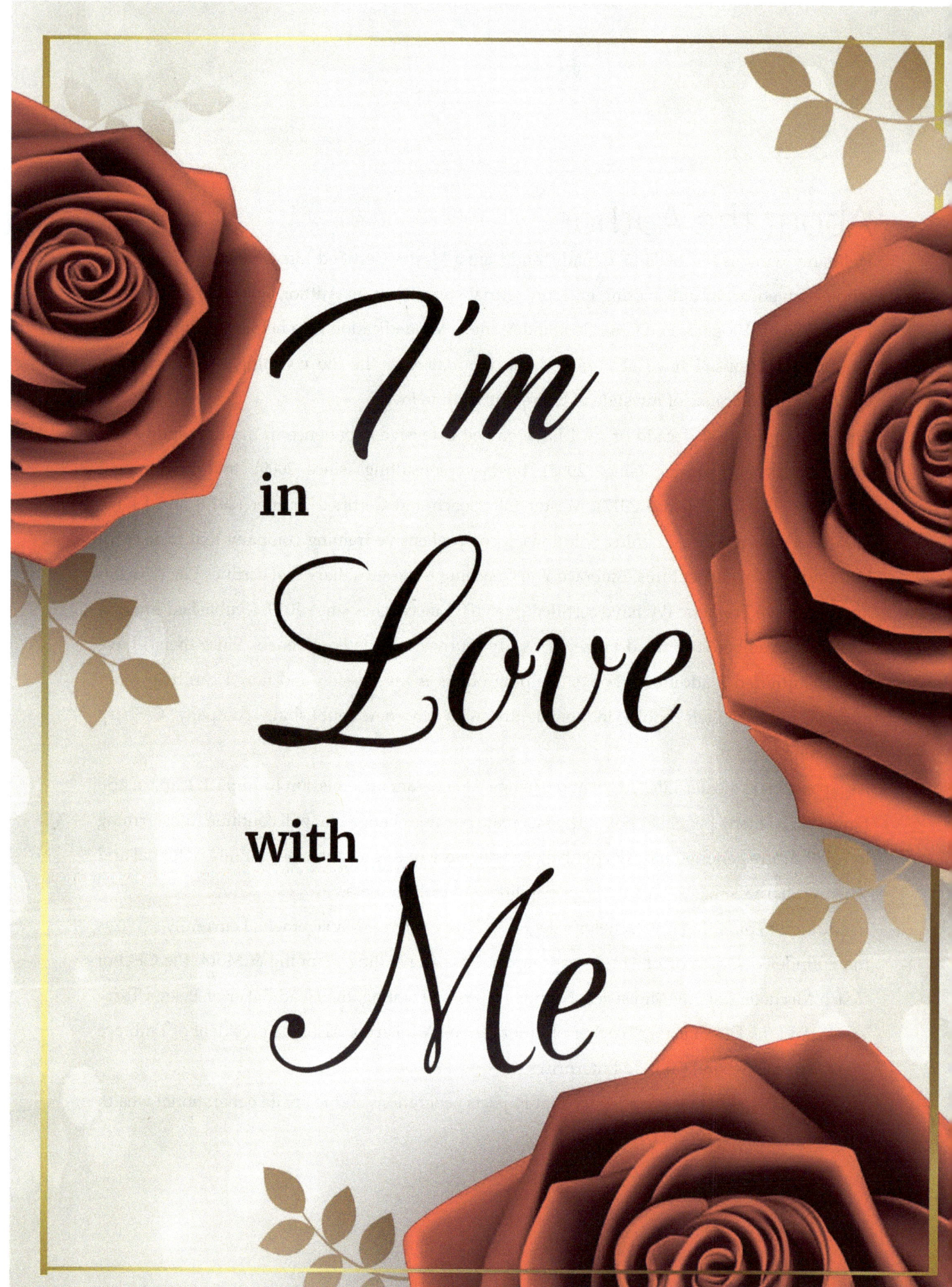

Day 1 Learn Your Love Language

Love is a language spoken by everyone, but we often have difficulty communicating our love to those we are in a relationship with. Most of us do not know what we need from those we are in relationship with because we are unknowing of what we need for ourselves.

In this journey to self-love, there is no better place to start than with learning your love language. By learning your love language, you will be able to better identify how to speak or communicate love to others and how to receive love from others.

What we love we should protect and treat with high esteem. We do things to make sure we preserve the thing we love because we love them. Those things we love less, we value less. We take less care; we do not always protect it. The same thing goes for us. When you love yourself and value yourself, you will protect yourself, treat yourself with love and hold yourself at high esteem. But when you do not love yourself, you will allow others to use and abuse you, disrespect you and disregard your value.

You may not have learned to love yourself as a child or you may have found yourself in a low place. It is not too late to start today. So, on this journey to self-love, learning the language of love will lead you through the rest of the journey.

To be better in relationship with others we must first work to master relationship with ourselves.

Gary Chapman in his book titled The 5 Love Languages states, "People express and receive love in 5 different ways called love languages: quality time, words of affirmation, gifts, act of service and physical touch. The sooner you discover your language and that of your loved one, the sooner you can take your relationship to new heights." This starts with your relationship with you.

1. Words of Affirmations: Love is expressed through words.
2. Physical Touch: Love is expressed through touching and togetherness.
3. Gifts: Love is expressed through the giving and receiving of gifts.
4. Quality Time: Love is expressed through spending alone time.
5. Act of Service: Love is expressed through doing kind things

Self-Love Exercise: Based on the definitions, identify what's your primary and secondary love language. Start thinking about ways you can display love to you. How can you show self-love through your love language?

Start thinking of people you are in relationship with who you may need to have a conversation with to teach them how to love you. People will love us according to how we teach them.

Self-Love Journal Exercise: On the next page, there is a self-love chart created by Ven King. It gives you some examples of ways to use your Self-Love Language. Review the list and journal your thoughts and feelings. Journal ways you can start demonstrating your love for you utilizing your love language. Make a list of at least 4 ways. Act starting today, then journal your commitment to speaking love and acting in love.

What's Your Self-Love Language?

CREATED BY VEX KING — AUTHOR OF 'GOOD VIBES, GOOD LIFE'

Quality Time

Scheduling some uninterrupted alone time to nurture your being.

- Meditation or introspection
- Transformational breathing
- Engaging in a creative passion
- Taking yourself on a date
- Reading a book or watching something
- Enjoying a warm beverage and blanket
- Spending time in nature
- Rest, recovery and sleep

Acts of Service

Doing tasks that need to completed or things that have been neglected, which serve your wellbeing.

- Cleaning your home
- Making your bed
- Taking the trash out
- Preparing healthy meals
- Scheduling, planning, organizing and delegating
- Attending therapy or coaching
- Living more purposely

Physical Touch

Honouring your body by doing things that make it feel good.

- Yoga, exercise, dancing, Qigong, etc
- Massage or spa day
- Epsom salt bath or warm shower
- Skin care and grooming
- Pampering sessions

Receiving Gifts

Treating yourself or creating gifts for yourself that spark joy.

- Spending money on your hobbies
- Shopping for things you love (within your means)
- Going on a trip or holiday
- Eating healthy food out
- Buying a nourishing smoothie
- Investing in knowledge and education
- Using arts and crafts to make yourself something

Words of Affirmation

Positive self-talk, gratitude towards yourself and empowering affirmations.

- Making a list of your strengths and successes
- Speaking kindly to yourself
- Journalling and mantras
- Speaking your ideal future into existence
- Little pep talks

Inspired by Gary Champman's 'The 5 Love Languages.' For more information on self-love, please read 'Good Vibes, Good Life.'

Vex King

Day 2 I AM ENOUGH

One day I was at work talking with my good friend Taylor. As we were talking, she was sharing her journey to receiving her master's degree and one of her professors was teaching about the "Imposter Syndrome. She was sharing with me the information and the book they were reading on the Imposter Syndrome, and it really hit home. She described the feeling I felt after every great moment in my life. I had never even heard of such a syndrome, so I wanted to know more about it.

The definition of the Imposter Syndrome is a psychological pattern in which an individual doubt their accomplishments and has a persistent internalized fear of being exposed as a fraud. I looked it up because I have experienced this feeling many times. I found myself at my lowest when I should have been at my highest because of a great accomplishment. I needed to understand why in my success I felt like an imposter. Research states that Imposter Syndrome is most common in those who are high achievers.

No matter how much external validation I received it never soothed the imposter in me. No matter how many compliments I received it didn't quiet the imposter in me. No matter how many people shared with me the transformation they received through my works, it never transformed me, and I felt like an imposter. It's not what others say to you that matters, it's what you say to you that matters most.

I bought two of the books Taylor recommended Impostor Syndrome (The Arcadia Project) by Mishell Baker and Lean In Women, Work, and the Will to Lead by Sheryl Sandberg, and those books assisted and empowered me to learn how to stand in my success because I AM ENOUGH!!

In past times, my inner critic made me feel unworthy to be celebrated. According to my inner critic, I was not enough. But after reading and soul searching, I decided to start affirming myself and whenever my inner critic tells me I am not worthy, I would boldly tell myself, "I AM ENOUGH". If I can work hard and put forth the time and effort needed to accomplish my goal, then I am worthy of the victory.

Many of use struggle from with knowing that we are enough because we spend so much time comparing what we have to what others have. But know that you have been given everything that you need to be what you have been created to be. You are complete and you are enough. Tell yourself I AM Enough.

I wrote it on a sticky note and put it on my mirror to remind myself that I AM ENOUGH. Daily as I go to the bathroom and look at myself in the mirror that sticky note is a constant reminder that I am victorious and worthy of every success I achieve and so are you.

Do not allow the voice in your head to make you feel less than enough. You are fearfully and wondrously made. You can be everything you have been created to be. YOU ARE ENOUGH.

When you know that you are enough you stop settling for less than enough in every area of your life. Things may not be perfect, but you are always going to be enough. Settling is not an option. Enough is Enough because you are enough.

Self-Love Exercise: Write on a sticky note I AM ENOUGH. Place it somewhere that you will see it daily. As often as you pass by it, read it aloud to yourself. Whenever your imposter shows up tell yourself, I am ENOUGH.

Self-Love Journal Exercise: Write about a time when you felt like a failure in your success. Write about your thoughts you are feeling. It is important to first identify the behavior to fix it. So, the next time you are feeling unworthy, love yourself enough to say aloud I AM ENOUGH!!!!

Free Compliment
PLEASE TAKE ONE

- Your hair looks really nice.
- You are quite lovely.
- You made someone smile today.
- You rocked today.
- I love those shoes.
- What you are doing matters.
- You are a good friend.
- You are special.
- You deserve a piece of chocolate.
- You are smart.

Day 3 Compliment Yourself

I was talking with my daughter Victoria in the car on the way to church one Sunday and I complimented her on how beautiful she looked, and she said, "Ma, I don't really know how to take compliments from people." That made me think back to the time when I did not know how to take compliments from people either. Whenever people would compliment me, I would always give what I call a "counter-compliment." For example, I am a true bargain shopper, so I look great most times at an unbelievable price. The moment someone says, "you look super cute" my counter-compliment is "I only paid 20.00 for this outfit." My counter-compliment totally discounted the compliment and devalued the compliment. Think about how you respond when people compliment you. Does it make you feel uncomfortable, do you counter-compliment, or do you simply say thank you?

I discovered that I was not able to accept compliments from others because I never complimented myself. The lack of love for myself made we feel unworthy to be complimented so I cancelled it out with a statement to devalue whatever was said to me.

I had a conversation with myself and told myself, "the next time someone compliments you, know that you are worthy of the compliment so simply just say: THANK YOU." The first couple times I failed at it miserably. I kept trying until it no longer felt funny to hear myself say it. I also started complimenting myself aloud in the mirror. At first it felt so uncomfortable to compliment myself, but I kept doing it until I started believing it. Once it became a norm to me, it was easier for me to accept compliments from others. I can now simply say "Thank You."

Self-Love Exercise: Go to the mirror right now. Look at yourself and think about how amazing you are. You may find this challenging at first but keep going. Find time in your day to compliment to yourself. After a while, this will become a daily habit. Remember to tell yourself I AM ENOUGH. On the next page is an activity sheet designed to help you identify things about you that are good qualities. From this activity you should be able to come up with five compliments. Write the compliments you come up with below and create a daily habit of complimenting yourself.

1.

2.

3.

4.

5.

Self-Love Journal Exercise: Journal how you felt when you were complimenting yourself. Think about the thoughts and feelings you felt while looking at yourself in the mirror. Write down those thoughts and feelings.

Things I like about my outward appearance
1.
2.
3.

Others like when I
1.
2.
3.

I'm unique because I can
1.
2.
3.

I am great at
1.
2.
3.

Challenges I have Overcome
1.
2.
3.

There are so many amazing things about you that you can admire daily

Day 4 Admire Yourself

Webster defines admire as "regard (an object, quality, or person) with respect or warm approval."

We live our lives in front of the world and it is easy to view the life of other people and pick out the things that you admire about them. We admire people for so many reasons. The problem is, we don't have access to the full details of what it took for them to become who or what they are. We spend countless hours watching the lives of others through social media; Influencers hand feed us the details of their life. Many of them pick and choose the details of their life to share and we compare our lives to the pictures they paint. This causes us to look at our lives and compare what is happening in real life to what is happening in social media.

Taking the time to get to know you better: loving you, is about learning yourself and being able to identify the many amazing qualities that you possess and cultivate them. I heard someone once say, "the grass is greener on the side you water the most."

Focusing on you and cultivating your gifts and talents will empower you to be the best version of you. I remember not being about to look at myself in the mirror because I didn't like the person I had become, but not anymore. Doing the self-work to become a better person has helped me and helped others who are around me. Feeling less than and not equal to those you admire can be a direct reflection of your inability to see how gifted, talented, artistic, smart, and simply amazing you are.

In my process, learning to love myself required me accepting myself, flaws and all. I also had to learn to be okay with who I am and to also accept who I am not. Once I started loving me for me, the lives of others became secondary. My focus shifted to me and doing the work on me that was needed. I started speaking positive affirmations aloud in the mirror and discovering qualities about me I can admire. The more I spoke it to myself the more I believed it, and, in the process, I identified how valuable I am to me and to the world.

Self-Love Exercise: Compile a list of 5 things you admire about you.

1.

2.

3.

4.

5.

Now, complete this sentence using your list above.

I admire me because I am:

_____

_____

_____

_____

Self-Love Journal Exercise: Journal your thoughts and feelings. Did you struggle to come up with a list? Was it hard completing your sentence?

Day 5 Invest in You

As a child, I was always told to be kind to others. To give to others first and take time to serve others. To be careful with my words to others because words hurt. This was good teaching because we should do all those things, but no one told me to be kind to myself. To be careful with what I said to me. To give to myself and serve myself. I wasn't taught to invest the same time and grace in me that I gave to others. So, I mastered being to others what I really needed to be to myself.

In 2009, I found myself empty with nothing left for me or anyone else. I had given all of me to everyone but gave nothing to myself. I was in an exceptionally low place; I was hopeless and felt worthless for years. It was not until 2012 I decided I was going to invest in me. I was going to give myself permission to invest in me. I discovered that I am at my best for others when I am at my best for me. I wanted to look better, feel better and be better. I wanted to do better with how I treated me, so I invested in me by way of therapy.

I discovered in a counseling session with my therapist that I needed to set time aside for me to be mentally and physically healthy. I loved to take bubble baths, so my therapist suggested that I included them in my daily schedule, and I made it a daily requirement for myself. It is okay for you to invest time in your day in you. I wanted to lose weight, so I hired a personal trainer. I started journaling my thoughts to get them out my head and I learned the good, the bad and the ugly about me and I embraced it. I learned that I

AM WORTH THE INVESTMENT and so are you. Start investing on becoming the best version of you.

Decide what that looks like for you. We are all different and so is the path to a better you. I can share with you what worked for me, but you have to decide what is going to work best for you. You may not enjoy a bubble bath daily, for you it might be a walk in the park or a run on the treadmill. Figure out what works for you.

Self-Love Exercise: Invest in yourself by doing daily self-care. Identify what you enjoy doing. What refreshes your soul? Identify what helps you to reset mentally, physically, and spiritually. If you are having trouble figuring it out here are some ways you can invest in, YOU!!

Meditate	Working Out
Reading self-help books	Make healthy meal choices
Drink more water	Minimize your screen time
Go for a walk	Spend time in nature
Get some rest	Taking a nap
Journaling	Coloring
Getting a therapist	Investing in a Life Coach
Socializing with friends	Take a trip

Self-Love Journal Exercise: Write out a plan on how you will invest more of your time in YOU!!!!

"To forgive is to set a prisoner free and discover that the prisoner was YOU"

– Lewis Smedes

Day 6 Forgive You

Have you ever been hurt? No, I mean like really hurt. I mean the hurt that just takes your breath away. I have more times than I can count. I was hurt repeatedly for years by someone who I loved for 19 years, and this hurt was inflicted all while saying they loved me. After 19 years of marriage, I found myself broken and feeling that it was not my fault. This left me angry; I thought I had the right to be angry and I wore it as a badge of honor.

After the separation, I was able to move pass the drastic change in my life I started to live again. Then one day my best friend asked me if I was over the hurt and my response was "Absolutely" and her follow up question changed the course of my life. She asked, "When you talk about it, does it still hurt?" I answered her yes, it will always hurt, and she said, "you're not over it if it still hurts and you haven't forgiven him."

That rocked my world and forced me to face the fact that I had imprisoned myself with unforgiveness. I realize that I was trapped and holding on to the pain of what happened to me. I was hurt rightfully so, but if I was going to be chained to the pain then I should save myself the trouble of starting over and just stay in the marriage.

I started on a journey to forgiveness and the more I forgave, the better I felt. I started looking inwardly to figure out what part I played in my pain? I wanted to figure out how I helped him hurt me? At what point did I stop being a victim and started being a participator? In this process, I discovered I needed to take ownership of my part in the failure of the marriage. Even though much of the hurt in the marriage wasn't done by me, I allowed myself to be hurt over and over again by staying in the marriage. Not only was I not a victim but a willing participant. Acknowledging my part made me want to say, "why did I stay?" The same strength to leave in year 19 was always in me, so why did I stay. I wasn't a hostage in the marriage. I chose to stay. I concluded that it was my lack of self-love that made it okay for me to stay in a marriage that was so toxic.

Prior to leaving, I remember having a conversation with myself. I asked myself this question, "will you be okay being in this same place you are in right now 20 years from now?" Initially I was so puzzled by this question, I then followed up with this statement "because you are in the same place you were in 20 years ago." I am not okay with doing this another 20 years!!! This cleared up all my confusion and ignited my desire to do something to change my situation.

Forgiveness is not for the person who did you wrong it is for you. Carrying the anger, guilt and pain is heavy on your heart and can show up in every area of your life. Trying to make them pay for what they did to you keeps you revisiting the place of pain over and over again. Forgiveness is a choice. You must decide to truly forgive not just in words but in deeds. You do not just wake up and it is done, you must decide to do the work to forgive. Forgiveness is a process and sometimes you have to work at it. It is like taking off the chains that have you bound to discover you chained yourself. Forgiveness frees you to live and to breathe again. It is like taking the weights off and being able to progress in life. Forgiveness is like releasing yourself from the prison of pain you have yourself locked in. The first step to forgiveness for me started with me forgiving me. I had to first forgive me for allowing him to hurt me and forgive him for hurting me in order to prepare my heart for the future.

Forgiveness is like a pardon. The person is guilty of the act, and you know they are guilty, but you make a conscious decision to release yourself of the burden of making them pay for what they did. It doesn't negate the fact that they are guilty, but you are free to move from the place of pain.

Self-Love Exercise: The first step to walking in forgiveness and no longer being chained to your pain is simply to forgive yourself. Often, we hold ourselves hostage. There is a hostage situation, and you are both victim and villain. So, take some time and start to think about the things and areas in your life where you need to simply forgive YOU. It is difficult to really love you if you have not forgiven you.

In my book Frozen: My Journey to True Forgiveness, I talk about a coaching model that I created The 3 A's. Accept, Acknowledge, Adjust. **Accept** the fact that you need to forgive you, **Acknowledge** what you could have done differently, and **Adjust** by taking the action to forgiving YOU.

Self-Love Journal Exercise: In your journal, write yourself an apology letter. Be specific about what you are apologizing for. This is going to be emotional, and it is going to require you to dig a little, but it will be well worth it. Once you are done with your letter destroy it and don't revisit that place of unforgiveness anymore.

Bonus Exercise: The next time you need to forgive, below is a strategy I use to forgive and grow. Give yourself the grace to forgive. Grace is unmerited and unearned favor. This gives you a plan to forgive.

Steps for me to Forgive & Grow

Own It – What was my part and what was their part.

Acknowledge It – Sit in your feelings and acknowledge your feelings.

Say It – Say out loud to yourself what it is you need to forgive.

Forgive It – Pardon the wrong that was done. Unchain yourself from it.

Learn From It – Identify the lesson you learned from the situation

Now Grow In Grace

"YOU NEVER FULLY SEE HOW TOXIC A PERSON REALLY IS UNTIL YOU WALK AWAY FROM THEM AND YOU CAN BREATHE."

Day 7 Rid Yourself of Toxic People

Looking back at life from 1993-2012, I did not realize how toxic my life was until I was divorced. It did not dawn on me how the toxic situation I was living in had crept into every space in my life. My physical, mental, emotional, and financial life had all become toxic. I became toxic not by what I did but by what I did not do. I have discovered that when you do not protect yourself from toxic people, places, and things, you give the toxicities access to consume you.

The most dangerous and one of the deadliest, are the toxins that seep in undetected. The ones that come in and you did not see them, feel them, or even smell them. By the time you realize what has happened, it is too late, and you are already exposed.

These toxins come into our life in many ways. One of the ways is by being connected to toxic relationships. When you are in a relationship you become what they are whether you want to or not. It is impossible for you to jump in water without getting wet and in the same way you cannot be in relationship with a toxic person without becoming toxic.

When I decided to end my first marriage, it was because I realized how deadly it was to my well-being. Once I was no longer connected for the first time since being a teenager, I could breathe.

The haze of toxicity that hovered over my life dissipated. I could finally breathe again. Life became one fresh breath after the other. Removing myself from the toxic relationship allowed me to see life differently. Finally, I could breathe.

Loving me enough to end a marriage I had been in for 19 years was not easy, but definitely worth it.

Self-Love Exercise: Start to examine your ties, covenants, connections in every area of your life. Toxic by definition is- Capable of causing death, exhibiting symptoms of infections, extremely harsh, malicious, or harmful relating to or being an asset that has lost so much value that it cannot be sold on the market. Causes something to be devalued. If you find any of these things present in your current relationships, reconsider it and what is it costing you to be connected. Love yourself enough to detox from your toxic connections.

Self-Love Journal Exercise: Start to create a detox in your life and space. A detox is a regimen or treatment intended to remove toxins and impurities from your body, mind, and spirit. Write out in your journal.

1. What is toxic in your life?

2. Who is toxic in your life?

3. Who makes you feel like you are suffocating when you are around?

4. Who are you connected to that cost you more just be connected to them?

5. Who contaminates your peace?

After taking time to journal your answers write out a plan to detox.

Day 8 Examine Your Connections

My mother grows flowers. She truly has a green thumb. It is like she can take one leaf off any plant and grow another plant from it. She is the only person I know who can take the plants you get from the funeral and grow them. My mom has plants in her front room that she has had for twenty years. They just keep growing and growing until they hit the roof of the house. She has mastered the art of growing plants.

She loves her plants. She talks to them, feed them and she has even given them names. She gives them bottled water and placed them out to get sun and rainwater. She really treats them like they are her children.

You may be thinking what does my momma having a green thumb have to do with examining connections? In her process of loving her plants she realized that as much as she loves them there is a time before the next season that she must prune the leaves that are no longer suitable for the next season. So, in your Journey of Self-Love, it is time to start to examine your connections.

There are connections that are not fit for the you that you are becoming. My momma did not just cut any and every leaf on the plants, but she examines to see which ones are no longer green and no longer growing. She looks to see which leaves have already died and are not vibrant and flourishing. Those are the ones she cuts and where she cuts them is strategic. She cuts them off without causing damage to the plant so that the growth is not affected for the next season.

There will be connections in your life that you will need to cultivate and help them grow. When my mom completes the pruning of her plants, she would take time to care for the plant to create an environment for growth. She would turn the dirt to stir up the nutrients, she adds more dirt and fertilizer to give the plants the additional minerals needed to grow for the next season. Relationships that are healthy or just needs a little help growing, see how you can fertilize and build those connections up to be a vital relationship that adds value and will help to propel you to the next dimension in your life.

Love yourself enough to disconnect and prune your connections so that you are not frustrated and weighed down with bad and toxic connections. Create an atmosphere of growth in those relationships that will help you in the next season of your life.

It is vital that you examine and understand the importance of this in your life. Holding on to people who should be cut off will stop you from growing at the pace you can grow. They will continue to suck up nutrients you need for you. They have no benefit to you and can even be detrimental to you. What helped you in the last season can kill you in the next season.

Love yourself enough to do a true evaluation of who you are connected to, and if they fit your future. If they do not love you according to the standard you have set for you in this season do not be afraid let them go.

Self-Love Exercise: Write down your top ten qualities. Write down your top five connections. Start to analyze your connections to see if your top five exemplifies any of those qualities. Do your top five connections build up your qualities or tear them down? Do they add value to your life? This reflection should start you to thinking about who you should keep and who you must disconnect from. Now start having the conversation with those individuals and actually disconnect.

Self-Love Journal Exercise: Now that you have done the pruning it is time to cultivate. Create a plan to enhance the connections you are going to keep. Write what you can do to cultivate the connection. Write out how they add value to you and how you can add value to them.

Day 9 Set Healthy Relationship Boundaries

Boundaries are like laws put in place to keep you safe. Boundaries are set out of love and not hate. Boundaries are for the protection of everyone involved. In life, it is especially important to set healthy relationship boundaries to keep your heart safe. Just as there are laws of the land put in place, there should be laws for your life. When I accepted who Mechelle had become, I realized it was because I had no boundaries in my life to keep me protected from hurt harm or danger. Those who I was connected to in my life had free reign in how they handled me, treated me, and dealt with me in most relationships.

I gave to those who I love and those I led 100% of me. You may be thinking why is this wrong to give 100% of you? Well, if you are giving 100% of you to others what is left for yourself? I found myself in the lowest point in my life completely empty. I served others at the highest level within my power because I thought it was right. I thought I was doing something great by being always all in. Any time people would ask me to do something, whether I wanted to or not I did it. I do not know how to do anything normal. Everything about me has always been extra. "I have even been called extra for no reason at all" and it is the truth. So, I gave, gave, and gave until I was completely empty. Once I empty, I also found myself alone. I could not call on any of those people who I gave all of me to for help. Because it was all about what I could give to them with no reciprocation.

In Good Boundaries and Goodbyes by Lysa Terkeurst, she stated "love should be unconditional, but access shouldn't be." Once I had come to my senses, I realized I needed to put boundaries in place so that I never get back in that place ever again. I knew I did not want to feel the way I was feeling, and I also knew for me to not be in that place again, I needed to do things differently.

The first change I implemented was the word "NO." NO is a complete sentence. No does not require anything else. No reason or explanation is required unless

I desire to give one. I walked around most of my life feeling overwhelmed because I said yes when I knew I should have said no. I was a people pleaser who also struggled with rejection. I thought I had to say yes for people to like me. If I said no, they would not like me or even love me. I had that sister-girl superwomen mentality. I was really trying to be every woman, but I had nothing left for me. I was the go-to girl, the one everyone called on but when I needed me for me, I could not show up for me.

We are granted grace for our life. We are given what is needed to be able to carry the weight of our on personal trials. We get in trouble when we take on other's issues, problems, and trials as our own because we are not graced to carry it. You are supposed to care, but not carry it. So, give them back their stuff.

Secondly, I set standards for what was going to be acceptable and what would not be for me. I set relationship boundaries, boundaries for my family and for myself. These standards served as boundaries. These standards helped me to safeguard my heart from mistreatment from others and from myself. In Good Boundaries and Goodbyes, Lisa also said "unchecked misuse leads to abuse." Any form of abuse is no longer acceptable. Be intentional about having the conversation about what your new boundaries are and the ramifications for crossing them. Again, unchecked boundaries lead to abuse.

Lastly, I realized that I set the standard, the laws, and boundaries for my life. Once I set the expectation of what was acceptable, people started realizing that to be in my space they had to govern themselves accordingly. I was unapologetic about my boundaries. They are non-negotiable.

In this journey to learning self, you will quickly learn that self-preservation is the key to loving you. Love yourself enough to take care of your well-being first. When you fly on an airplane, the pilot comes across the intercom system and gives instructions. One of the instructions he gives is if the oxygen mask comes down, you are instructed to put your mask on first and then help others. You are no good to others if you are not alive. Love those around you enough to love you first.

Protect yourself by putting up those healthy boundaries and do not sacrifice yourself trying to preserve others.

The definition of boundary is where I end, and you begin. Set boundaries, healthy boundaries by guarding your heart.

Self-Love Exercise: Answer the following questions

- Think about the areas in your life you feel most overwhelmed in. Write them down.

- Think about the people in your life that leave you feeling exhausted. Write their names down.

- Think about the last time you said yes when you knew you should have said no. Write it down.

- Think about the people in your life that do not add value to the connection. Write their names down.

- Think about the people currently in your life who do not value the space you have created in your life for them. Write their names down.

These are the relationships you need to establish boundaries with consequences.

Self-Love Journal Exercise:

Take some time and write out your thoughts and feelings about the answers to the above questions. Take time to write out how you can do things differently when it comes to establishing boundaries. Write out the needed conversations so that you can start establishing good boundaries or say goodbye.

Write out your NO statement- the next time someone is requiring more of you than you are willing to give them. Remember NO is a complete sentence. It requires nothing else. No reason, No explanation.

Day 10 Show Up for You

I have come to the realization that always being available for others can leave you too tired to fight for yourself. I found myself in that place. I was so busy being present for everyone else that I could not be present for me. I needed me and I had nothing left of me to give me.

In 2009, I realized I was empty and depressed. I needed to stop giving so much of me out to others and start practicing self-preservation. Definition of self-preservation. 1: preservation of oneself from destruction or harm. 2: a natural or instinctive tendency to act to preserve one's own existence. So, in other words SAVE YOU FIRST.

Again, when you are flying the captain will come over the intercom and will instruct you. "If your oxygen mask comes down, APPLY YOURS FIRST and then help others." If you are no good to you then you are no good to anyone else.

We have been given a measure of grace for what we must go through and what we must endure. We become overwhelmed and are unable to show up for ourselves when we have taken on the problems, issues, and responsibilities of others. You have not been equipped to take on the problems of others. You can be there to show support and help others through what they are going through, but it is not your job to take on the burdens of others. You can care without carrying. When carrying the weight of others, it leaves you no room to carry your own. When it is time for you to fight for yourself, you will have no fight left. Love yourself enough to save some of you for you.

In order to be present for you during those dark rainy days, you must make sure you are taking care of you. Make sure you are mentally stable enough to be present in your own situation. Have you ever been so loaded down with the problems of others that when your storm started raging you felt like you were sinking and just gave up on your struggle? You could not fight your fight because there was nothing left. You really needed you and there was nothing left. You were like an empty cup. Are you at the point of giving up on you because you feel you cannot fight anymore? **Do not lay down on the fight!! Remember the definition** of self-preservation is a natural or instinctive tendency to act to preserve one's own existence. Do not give up SHOW UP FOR YOU. Give people back their problems. You are not responsible to take on their issues as your own. It's too heavy for you to carry yours and theirs. You have been graced for yours; not theirs.

Self-Love Exercise:

Here are five suggestions on how to start showing up for you. Review them repeatedly until they become a part of your thought process.

Step 1- Start from today.
Step 2- Give everybody back their own problems, you do not have the grace for it.
Step 3- Don't try pouring from an empty vessel.
Step 4- Only give to others from your overflow
Step 5- Create a plan to reset when needed so you can fill yourself back up again.

Self-Love Journal Exercise:

Take a few minutes and think about the ways you have overextended yourself to others. After taking some time to think about it, start writing a promissory note to yourself to not give to others what you need to keep for you. Promise yourself to always look out for you and be there for you in the times that you need you. It's okay to say no I can't and mean it.

Bonus Exercise: Think about where your vessel is right now at this moment. Write your name on the vessel because it represents you. Shade in the level your vessel is right now. You may discover that you really have nothing to give not even to you.

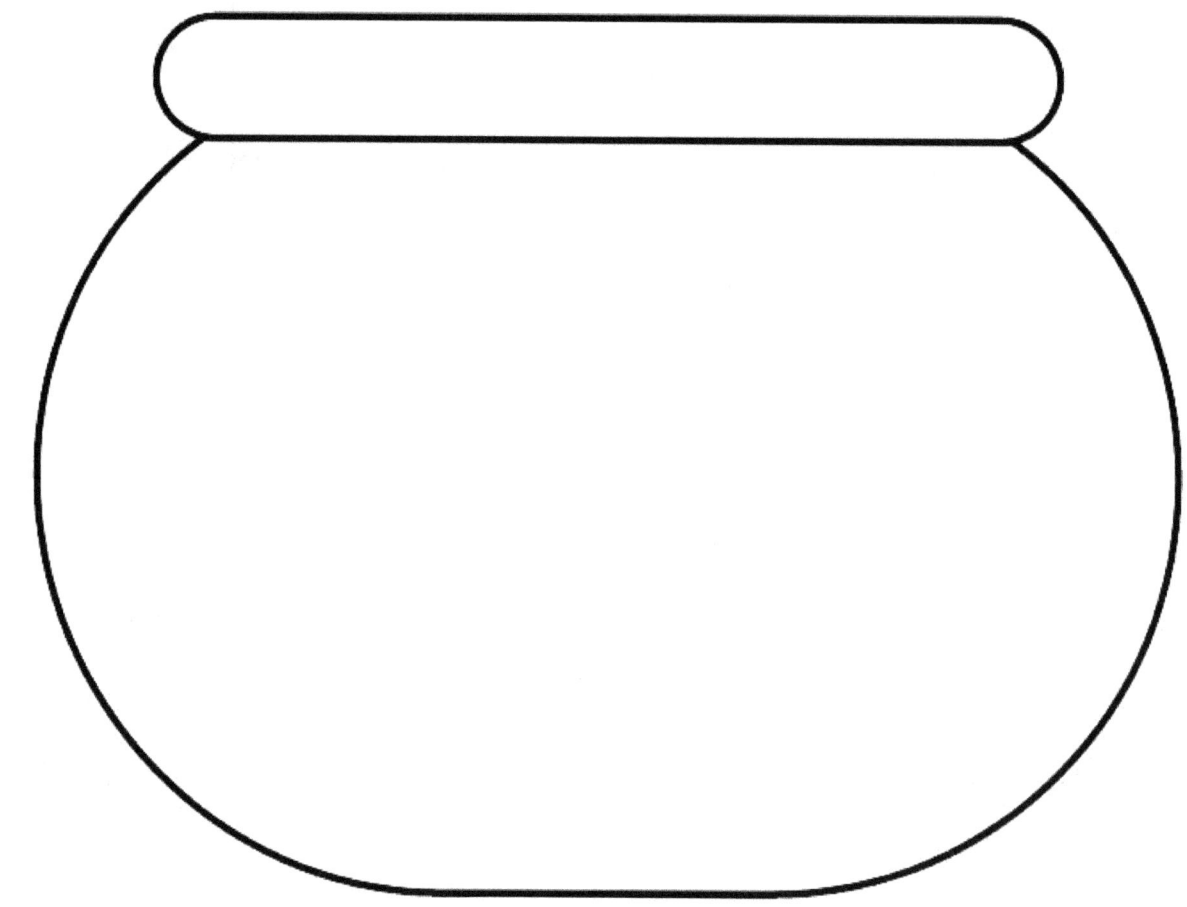

Day 11 You Can't Unhappen It

Living in regret of your past decisions can hold you hostage to those decisions. Decisions you made, where you went, what you did, who you loved, and who you didn't love will plague your right now. Past failures will deflate your esteem. It will cause you not to trust your own decisions; make you not want to try again.

Past mistakes you made will affect the way you deal with people in your current relationships. You will really damage your present by the past hurts and disappointments. You will also damage healthy relationships if you handle the person as if they are the person from the past. You cannot UNHAPPEN IT. Hurts of your past that are left unhealed will cause you to reenact it into your present.

I personally have made some not so smart decisions in my life. Some plain ole dumb decisions. Decisions that my family and friends told me not to make, and I did them anyway and paid dearly for not listening to the people who loved and cared about me. All decisions have consequences and repercussions. To be honest, I am still paying for some of those decisions today, but I have been able to move forward by forgiving myself and learning lessons from my mistakes. I realize that there is nothing I can do that will allow me to go back and change what I did. I cannot UNHAPPEN it and neither can you.

If you break a glass and then glue it back together, no matter how perfectly you glue it together, you will still see the cracks. It might hold water the same as it did before it was broken but you cannot unbreak it. This is the way your bad decisions of your past are. You get past them, but the damage is still there.

You are here today because you survived the mistakes you made; stop revisiting it. You can't heal what you keep replaying over and over again. You can't UNHAPPEN IT. But even if you are still broken that doesn't make you useless. Broken crayons still color. You can be made whole again, but you cannot UNHAPPEN what was done. If it didn't kill you don't let the thought of it kill you. Letting those hurts of your past go can be your greatest testimonies. Let God get the glory out of it because it is working for your good. Nothing is wasted with God, not even your mistakes.

I was able to forgive myself and get past my not-so-great decisions in life by applying a simple practice called the 3A's Accept, Acknowledge, and Adjust.

I had to Accept the fact that I could not go back and change what has already happened. I can't UNHAPPEN it. Accept the fact that I needed to make better choices and Accept the fact that I did not make the best decision for my future.

Secondly, Acknowledge is the next step. I needed to take ownership of my part in the failure of my marriage. Again, even though I was not the one doing the cheating, lying, stealing, he was, but I had a part in it because I allowed him to continue to do those things to me over and over again. I did not stop him from hurting me, I helped him hurt me. I was not a victim I was a willing participant. Once I acknowledged I was a part of the problem, partly at fault, I looked at my situation differently.

Adjust is the last and ultimate step. Once I had accepted that change needed to happen, acknowledge what went wrong and my part in it, I now needed to do something about it. My adjustment was seeking healings. I realized I could not get healed the same place I was hurt. I needed to heal despite my fear of the unknown or my fear of what will happen next; I had to change my environment. I created an exit strategy plan. I packed up and moved on the date I planned. The adjust process is the "DO SOMETHING" phase. I realized that I can't UNHAPPEN it, so I needed to do something about it. You can do the same by Accept, Acknowledge, Adjust!!!

Self-Love Exercise: Go to the mirror look yourself in the eyes and tell yourself "YOU CAN'T UNHAPPEN IT." Now on a sticky note write it out and put it on your mirror as a reminder.

Self-Love Journal Exercise: Think about the past decision you regret making the most that holds you back from progressing. Whenever you attempt to move forward this decision stops you in your tracks. You can't UNHAPPEN it. Included on the next page is a journal page to write it out. let's do the work. ACCEPT, ACKNOWLEDGE, ADJUST. Regret should only be a reference point and not a guide. This is one of the Coaching models I use to get past when I am stuck. Be open and honest with yourself so you can forgive and move forward. If you need more space don't hesitate to finish on the journal pages in the back.

The 3 A's

Accept – What happened?
_____
_____
_____
_____

Acknowledge – What was your part in what happened?
_____
_____
_____
_____

Adjust – What can you do to move forward?
_____
_____
_____
_____

Day 12 Know Who Your Friends Are

Putting people in the proper place in your life will alleviate many disappointments experienced in relationships with people. There are times when you have people in spaces in your life who are not providing you with what you currently need. We become very frustrated when we have people in the wrong place of our life. Expectations are established by roles. We have people in wrong places and in roles they don't have the capacity to fulfill. We lose good people because we become frustrated with the unmet expectations that the roles bring. I want to introduce to you a concept that has helped me to take a closer look at the people in my life and evaluate if they are in the right place according to their actions and not according to their title.

I place people in one of the three circles or spheres they fall into. These three circles are Followers, Fans, Friends.

Let us define the three roles. First Followers- those who trail you from a distance. They "follow" you on social media, they like your post from time to time, and occasionally comment on your post, but nothing else. If you have not identified that the person is a follower only you might find yourself disappointed and feeling unsupported if you are looking for them to show up at an engagement or purchase your product. You will find yourself discouraged if you are looking for all the people who "follow" to be present for you. They do not have your heart nor vision in mind so do not be mistaken in thinking they will do anything other than "follow" you from a distance. They do not provide real support they only provide numbers. They never provide real engagement, but they are maintaining a watch on what you are doing. They will not show up for you, will not be significant in any way in your life, they are just around. Your followers will also watch to report to those who do not have access to watch. Does this sound like anyone you know? Followers have no benefit, but they are needed. They will keep your count up for people who are watching.

Secondly, Fans- Webster defines a fan as an enthusiastic devotee usually a spectator. Now Fans are more interactive than followers. They want to have a closer seat in the arena of your life. They will support you, but the support is limited. They will show up for the easy stuff. They show up when things are going well in your life. You may never meet them in real life, you only know the basics about them. From time to time, you may see one and they will often say to you "I have been watching you from a distance, but nothing more should be expected. They just want to watch. If they can gather from you what they want or what they need they are around, but they are not willing to do no heavy lifting. You can only give them access to your pretty picture. Your fans will show up at your event, but that's just it. They will just show up!! They will tell someone about your product, but they won't buy it themselves. Identify those who are your Fans. It is important to help you put them in perspective in your life. They may not invest money, but they will definitely invest time. You must know their capacity as a Fan will limit the frustration and disappointment that comes with failed expectations. When you are expecting more from people than they are willing to give or have the capacity to provide, you end up hurt and disappointed every time. Fans will watch you daily; keep track of what you are doing closely. They will mimic what you do. They desire the appearance of being close to you without the work required to be close to you.

Let me pause here and say your role in a person's life may not be their role in your life. So, be clear in what role people play in your life to avoid ending good relationships due to misplacement. You are a benefit to your fans, and they want others to know they are associated with you because it makes them look and feel supported, but you won't get the same benefit from them.

Lastly, Friend- Webster defines a friend as a person whom one knows and with whom one has a bond of mutual affection. So, in an essence to be a friend there needs to be a mutual bond or mutual affection. These are the people who support you like you support them; they participate in your life, they show up for you when you need them, they support what you do. Not only do they want to see you win they will help you win. We put a lot of people here who are not worthy of the role. We don't see this as a vital role in our life, so we don't take it seriously. Friends should be people you have found to be safe. What do I mean by safe? They can be trusted with the you that the followers and fans never get to see. Now, don't get friends and friends on social media mixed up because they are not the same. You will get your feelings hurt bad if you get these two mixed up. We do not have a lot of people who fall in this category. The closer to you the smaller the circle should get. This is why it is possible to have 100,000 followers on social media and feel completely alone. We need friends in our lives who want nothing more from us than to be our friend. These are the ones that will tell you when you are wrong and help you see things from a different perspective. They will help get you back on track if you have fall off and they will cover you if you fall. These are the ones you can fall out with on Monday morning and they calling you at lunch to make a lunch date. Devoted friends are few far and between. Friends will allow you to be who you truly are and still love you for who you are. Friend is not a permanent position and should be reevaluated often. When your season changes your friends might too. You can still maintain relationship with people and reallocate their access to you.

Misplacement of people will cause you undue pain and suffering because you will expect something from them that they cannot give you. It is like putting a square peg in a circle it just does not fit. Putting people in the right places helps to set boundaries for you and them. Matthew 7:15-20 tells us to judge a tree by the fruit it bears. One major mistake we make is we don't really look at the fruit. Fruit don't lie. Take time to make sure the people in your life are in the right place. Followers, Fans, Friends.

Self-Love Exercise: List your top five people you communicate with on a regular basis and decide which category they fit in: Followers, Fans or Friends

1.

2.

3.

4.

5.

Self-Love Journal Exercise: Start to evaluate the roles that you play in the life of the people you listed above. Start to think more about the way you interact with them and journal your experience with them. This will help you identify the role you play in their lives. You may discover that you are in the wrong place in some people lives. This will help you set boundaries in your life.

Day 13 Know the Capacity of Those Around You

Loving you is learning how to protect yourself from undue stress, aggravation and frustration that comes from being in a relationship with yourself and relationship with others. We spend a lot of time and effort expecting from people what they do not have the capacity to provide. We also spend time inwardly frustrated not knowing or understanding our own capacity. Knowing your own capacity of what you can do, cannot do, can handle, and cannot handle is a must. We must know what triggers us to do good or what triggers us to shut down. Not having a good understanding of your thresholds brings about frustration when expectations are not met. Most disappointments are directly connected to the unmet expectations we have of people. When our expectations are not met, we are often disappointed, and our feelings get hurt. When we know the capacity, our expectations change.

If you have a gallon of water and a bottle of water, they both have water in them, but their capacity is different. You can easily pour a bottle of water into an empty gallon jug. That leaves a lot of room in the gallon jug to hold more water. But if you take a gallon of water and attempt to pour it into the water bottle it does not have the capacity to hold the water. This is how most of our connections are. We are the gallon of water and those in our circle is the bottle of water. You can handle their capacity with ease with room to spare, but they are unable to handle yours. This is why you have to be aware of how much of you that you give to those in your circle. When we expect ordinary people to perform at an extraordinary level we are let down. We expect from people what we give to them. Well, they do not always have the capacity to give that back to us and because they don't, we find ourselves irritated, agitated, frustrated.

When we expect ordinary people to give back to us the extraordinary that we have given them it doesn't happen. They do not have the ability to provide to you what you gave to them. I remember at one point in my life I was extremely disappointed in people. I had given so much of me with little in return. I took on the motto of no expectation, no disappointment. This allowed me to accept people for who they are. To see people for their truth and not my idea of who they are. This is why we must evaluate our connections because our needs change from season to season. Seasons change. What was good for you in one season may be detrimental in the next season. Ecclesiastes 3:5 there is a time to embrace and a time to refrain from embracing. Always know what season you are in.

Once I started to live by the no expectations; no disappointment mantra, I could truly see people for who they really are, and I can meet them where they are. We expect to meet people in the place of extraordinary because that's where we are, but they are not where we expected them to be because they are at ordinary. So, get rid of the preconceived notion of what people should give back to you for what you have given to them. This will change your life and set you free from the disappointment and hurt. No this does not free people from accountability. People must be held accountable for who they are, what they do and how they respond. This is why we need to be aware of what we can handle and what they can handle. Grant access to you based on a person's level of responsibility and make sure circumstances are in place. When someone shows that they cannot handle the responsibility of the access you have given them, you must adjust it to prevent you from being hurt.

Maya Angelou said, "when people show you who they are, believe them." We often see people in a different light than they really are, and we want better for people than they want for themselves. Just like you must acknowledge where you currently are, you also must acknowledge where the people around you currently are. Knowing the capacity of those around you takes away the undue expectation of people to be perfect and to always get it right but when there is no expectation there is no disappointment and you can love people for who they really are.

Self-Love Exercise: Write down on a sticky note "No expectations; No disappointments." Make it visible for you to see and as often as you need to remind yourself in those tough situations in relationship.

Self-Love Journal Exercise: take a moment and think about the last time you were disappointed by unmet expectations. Journal the following questions.

- Who was the person you were disappointed by?

- What was the situation that happened?

- How did it affect the access they had to you?

- Where are they now in your life?

Know how much of you to give to those around you. Everyone around you is not equipped to handle all of you.

Day 14 Everyone Can't Handle All of You

One day I was watching TEDx UNO video, and I came across a video titled "5 People You Need in Your Life to be Happy" by Stacey Flowers. This video talks about we are the average of the five people closest to you. This video really caused me to review those around me.

The five key people she discussed in the video are:

A **cheerleader** who roots you on

A **mentor** who points you in the right direction

A **coach** who helps to guide you

A **friend** who helps to comfort you

A **coworker** relates to you in your work or your field

These are known as your factor five. They do not actually have to be five people each, but the role is very important and has a purpose. We sometimes expect our best friend to be our all and when they cannot be, we are left disappointed with unmet expectations. Knowing the capacity of those around you is about knowing what part of you they can handle. Disappointment comes when expectations are not met. We do not expect a tree to be a dog, nor do you expect your dog to be a tree. Your expectations for the dog are to run, jump, bark, and the tree to produce shade, fruit and to be grounded. Now the same is with those around you; know them well enough to know how much of you they can handle. You may be thinking, "what does this have to do with me loving myself?" Let me say it absolutely is important to you loving. Love yourself enough not to give the wrong parts of you to the wrong people because it's damaging. Giving them what they can handle will help you guard your heart. It saves you disappointment, hard feelings and from ruining good relationships. You are not convinced yet? Okay, I got you. I have this friend and every time I have one of my brilliant ideas, I can call her, and she is going to tell me how wonderful my idea is, how smart I am and how no one in the world is as smart as me. She was my cheerleader and has been for years. I work in the fraud department of a national bank and sometimes my job was very stressful. I was riding home one day and decided to call her to vent about my day. I called her and I gave her an ear full and more. She quietly listened and said nothing the entire time I talked. Our conversation is never one-sided we interrupt each other and go back and forth, but this time it was different. Once I was finished all she said was WOW. Nothing else. I was completely lost and confused and a little bothered that our conversation did not go as planned. I ended the call with my friend, saying "I'll call you later." That left me disappointed with our friendship and in my mind, I was like I will not call her anymore.

From that one situation I was ready to write off our whole friendship. Simply because at that moment, it did not dawn on me that she was not able to take in what I was feeling in that moment and turn it into a "cheer moment." She didn't understand my frustration and could not relate to my pain. She could not cheer for me in that moment. I had never identified her as being my cheerleader, just my friend and by habit I called her and dumped a lot of stuff on her that was an overload she could not handle. The person I needed to call was a coworker. Someone with knowledge of what I was sharing and could empathize with me. In that moment I didn't need a "go friend go" I needed a "friend that is a stressful situation and tomorrow will be better."

So, it was not her fault, she was not equipped to handle the role of my co-worker, my venting was a lot to handle and understand. It was just outside of her capacity.

After taking some time to re-evaluate my circle and their capacity of the me they could handle, I am now more strategic with who I call when I'm in need and created boundaries and a plan for who to call when I need them.

Now, think about how many good friendships have been ruined by not knowing your friend's capacity and what part of you they can handle!!

Self-Love Exercise: Think about your factor five. The top five friends you have and list them below. These are your top five go to people. Those who you go to when things are good or bad, when you are happy or sad. The person you go to when you need someone to hype you up or calm you down.

1.   Cheerleader_____

2.   Coach_____

3.   Mentor_____

4.   Friend_____

5.   Coworker_____

Now from the five roles, identify what capacity you factor five serve you and list their name. next to the role.

The next time you need someone make sure you call the right one for the right job.

Self-Love Journal Entry: Think about your top five people in your inner circle and think about times when you did not get from them what you needed. Now examine their capacity and their roles. I mean really think about it.

Have you been attempting to get something they do not have the ability to give you because of their capacity?

Take some time to really think about this and you may discover that you may

have lost some friendships you need to go back and mend because you were wanting them to serve you in a capacity they were not equip to.

Day 15 Find Out What Centers You

In the age of technology, the most important accessory for your devices is your charger. Your charger has become essential to your life. Without the charger to charge your devices they are worthless. We all are very careful to keep up with our chargers because we want to always have the ability to use our very pricey devices.

Growing up there was an American Express commercial that said, "And never leave home without it." American Express created a whole marketing campaign around the phrase. It has been named amongst the eight most successful campaigns. That is the way we feel about our chargers, we never leave home without it. Because our devices are essential to our life, we feel we need to be connected. We always make sure to charge our device. When there is a new update for our devices, it always asks if it may restart your phone to get everything aligned and reset. In order for your device to function properly there are steps that you must take to ensure it continues to function at its optimum performance.

We take all these measures to make sure that when we need to use our devices, they are charged, but we fail to make sure WE are charged. We allow ourselves to get drained and run down. We allow ourselves to give out so much that we find ourselves on empty. When your battery is dead your phone is not good for use, and neither are you uncharged. It is necessary to stay charged up, so we are the best version of who we are.

I found myself empty in 2009. I had given out everything I had to give. I was so many things to so many people, I had nothing left to give to me. My life was out of alignment. Mentally, physically, and emotionally out of alignment. When we drive our car and it is out of alignment, it's hard to keep the wheel centered. This makes it difficult to drive and if you are not careful you will crash. Getting a wheel alignment makes it easier to stay on the road and keep the wheel in the middle. Just like your car needs and alignment, your life does too. We are of little value to others until we love ourselves enough to figure out what centers us. We need a heart alignment.

I went to see a therapist because I was on the verge of having another mental breakdown. He said to me "you need to take some time to center you. You are overextending yourself in what you give to others, and it is leaving nothing for yourself. If you do not do something to correct it, you are going to end up back in the mental hospital. You are everything to everybody and nothing to you." I just sat back in the chair and looked at him with tears in my eyes because he was right. I couldn't help but think to myself, "how did I get back here again?"

For me that was a big wake up call. When I was released from the mental hospital 5 years before, I promised myself I would never go back. This conversation left me trying to figure out how I got back here. With tons of questions and with no answers, I did not want to go through that again, so I needed to figure out how to fix it. I decided that I would start doing self-care and figuring out what centered me.

I realized that for much of my day my time was spent with people. My spouse, my kids, my church members, my employees and never just me. I started by carving out time in my day just for me. I discussed my need to have some ME time with my family and they helped me to navigate through it. I started journaling my thoughts and feelings to get it all out of my head and on paper.

Fast forward 10 years to now, I am working a full-time job and running my businesses full time. There are times that I feel myself getting low and I must take time to center me. I have started setting aside time to reset. My reset is what gets me balanced, centered, refilled and ready to take on the world. I have deemed Monday as my reset day. Now you may not be able to take an entire day to reset, but it is very necessary that you take time to center you. It is not the quantity of time but the quality of time.

I also do not just center my body, but my heart, mind, and soul. I center my spirit through corporate worship, meditation, prayer, and inspirational videos to help me center my soul and my spirit. This keeps my moral compass centered and keeps me on the right track in all areas of life. I have affirmations all around my house to keep me visually and mentally centered and reminded of my goals, mission, and tasks. I listen to audible books; I take long walks and do stretches while listening to scriptures and prayers.

Keeping you in the forefront of your life is not an easy task. We are taught to see about others and that seeing about us is selfish. We should put other's thoughts and feelings before our own and we should sacrifice of ourselves for others. We love others and esteem others higher than we do ourselves and the more we give to others the Godlier we are. This is incorrect and cannot be your way of life. If this is how you are currently operating, let me assure you that it is okay to say "no." Steward your yes because your yes is never free. Your yes cost you time you will never get back. Saying No, isn't selfish but necessary. We must practice self-preservation. Once again like when you are on the plane and the captain comes on the overhead and says, "in the event that the mask come down due to turbulence APPLY YOUR MASK FIRST AND THEN ATTEMPT TO HELP OTHERS." So, when it comes to your own self-care apply it to you and then apply it to others. Save you first.

Being centered is vital to your self-preservation. Take time to center you and get back to you. Getting to know what centers you is of the upmost importance and it needs to be a part of your daily routine. I recently started a health journey. My goal is to be Whole, Healthy, and Wealthy. I made the decision to put me first. Before I service anyone else workout for me. I have vowed to not do anything for anyone until I take time to do this for me. I have not felt this whole in so many years.

Self-Love Exercise: Go to the mirror, look yourself in the eyes and apologize for putting others first and not making sure you are good first. Have a conversation with you about making you a priority.

Self-Love Journal Exercise: Set a plan for 7 days to take time to reset and center you daily. Identify what that reset looks like. Here is a list of self-care regimens to help you center yourself and get recharged.

1. Pick one thing that you need to do and get it done so it is off your mental "to do" list.
2. Get a manicure or pedicure.
3. Get a massage.
4. Spend a few minutes each day learning something new.
5. Use a planner or a calendar to intentionally schedule "me time."
6. Listen to music that inspires.
7. Listen to a video that motivates you.
8. Drink calming tea and curl up with an enjoyable book.
9. Write a list of things you are grateful to have in your life and post it somewhere you can see it often.
10. Journal it out

You are a winner

You can

You are loved

You are a Finisher

You are Enough

Your are G R E A T

You are Qualified

You are already Equipped

WHAT YOU SAY TO YOU MATTERS MORE THAN WHAT OTHERS SAY TO YOU. SILENCE YOUR INNER CRITIC

Day 16 Silence Your Inner Critic

Growing up there was a cartoon titled GI Joe: The Great American Hero. At the end of the cartoon GI Joe would always end the show by saying, "knowing is half the battle." Many of us lose battles daily simply because we do not know that there is a battle going on. Knowing that you are in a fight is half of what is needed to win the battle. We lose our personal struggles in our minds because we do not understand that we don't have to lay down and lose but we can win. We are in a battle against our thoughts, against the words that have been said to us and words said by others to us. Knowing that there is a battle going on in your head is half of the battle. Your failures or your success begin in your mind first. Roy T. Bennett once said, "don't be pushed around by the fears in your mind." Do not allow your thoughts, failures, and the fear of failure to push you around. Do not allow the thoughts of failure and not actual failure dictate what you do. The battlefield in the mind is where most battles are fought, won, and lost, but if you do not know that you are warring against those words in your mind, you will lose every battle. The inner critic inside your head is always fighting against you with words you have said to you, or words other have said to you in your voice.

We are our biggest critics. We are harder on ourselves than anyone else. You must learn to silence the inner critic by speaking positive affirmations. You also must learn to give it a positive word to give to yourself. The more you rehearse the more positive words, more positive thoughts you will have and the more you will speak those positive words to yourself. We have an inner critic, but we also have an inner nurturer and the one you feed the most is the one that will speak the most. In 1 Samuel 30:6 David had to encourage himself, but spies in Numbers 13:33 saw themselves as grasshoppers.

Your inner critic is always telling you what you cannot do. What you are not ready to do and what you are not qualified to do. Telling you that you are a failure, you are a loser, and a fraud. Start today telling yourself "YOU CAN." You can take charge of what you are thinking. You are in full control of your thinking, even though you can't control your thoughts. Start declaring that you can do it, declaring that you will do it, declaring that you are winner, declaring that you will no longer lose. The power to silence your inner critic lies in you. You are already equipped for the assignment on your life. Tell yourself "Yes I Can." Whenever your inner critic tells you that you can't you remind it that you can because you are already equipped. You have the power to be everything you have been created to be. Be determined not to lose the battle in your mind before you fight the battle. Silence the inner critic and feed your inner nurturer. Managing your self-talk is key to the level of success you are able to achieve. You will never achieve beyond what you can see for yourself. Your inner critic is always going to tell you that you cannot, but you don't have to believe it. You have the power to decide today that you are going to stop being and start doing.

That moment when you think you have done an excellent job at something and then that voice in your head discounts your accomplishment fight back. That is the voice of your inner critic in your head. I gave my inner critic a name. Her name is Petty Penelope. I named her Petty Penelope because she is PETTY. She will pick me apart if I let her. I have felt like I was on the mountain top and by the time she is done being petty, I am in the valley. The words she says to me sometimes are hurtful and cruel. But I realize a lot of what she says to me sounds a lot like what other people have said to me. She repeats to me the unkind things that has been said to me, but she repeats it in my voice. So, what others have said to hurt me is now being used by me on me. She also repeats to me the things I have said about me. She repeats what she has heard others say to me.

We cannot control what comes to our mind, but we can control what we do with those thoughts. You cannot control your thoughts, but you can control what you think. You have to fight negative with the positive. Positive always wins. I was a victim of verbal abuse for many years and Petty Penelope reminds me of the things they said to me. I have to often times do like David did and encourage myself.

Here is the strategy I use to combat my inner critic. The first step to overcoming your inner critic is identifying the voice of your inner critic. Second step is when your inner critic speaks negative, you counter act it with positive words. This will neutralize the negative thought. Third step is managing your words. Control what you say to you because your inner critic will use your words against you. The key to winning is knowing that there is a battle going on. Knowing is half the battle and a winning strategy is the other half.

Self-Love Exercise: Throughout the day today, on the note card below keep track of all the negative thoughts that comes to your mind. Write them down and make notes of what you say to you.

Self-Love Journal: Getting to understand your Inner Critic is acknowledging the voice of your inner critic and combating the negative thoughts. From your list above, identify where it originated from. Was it something someone said to you or something you said to you. By identifying where it came from, you can cancel it at the root. This will help you to confront it and resolve it.

Bonus Exercise: Below is a list of positive affirmations you can use to feed your inner nurturer. This list of I Am, I Can and I Will affirmation. Use this list to combat the negative self-talk. Start saying them daily and watch how you will evolve into a higher version of you. Then you write down at least one of your own.

I Am affirmation

I Am Enough

I Am All Ready Equipped for what I am assigned to do

I Am someone's Answer

I Am beautifully and wondrously made

I Am Whole Healthy and Wealthy

I Will Affirmation

I will be the prosperous and successful

I will be the head and not the tail

I will be above only and not beneath

I will be all God created me to be

Because I Am Enough

I Can Affirmations

I can be whole by doing the work needed to become whole

I can do all that I am created to do

I can live a life of balance

I can unclutter my mind and my space will follow

I can walk with my head held high because I am enough

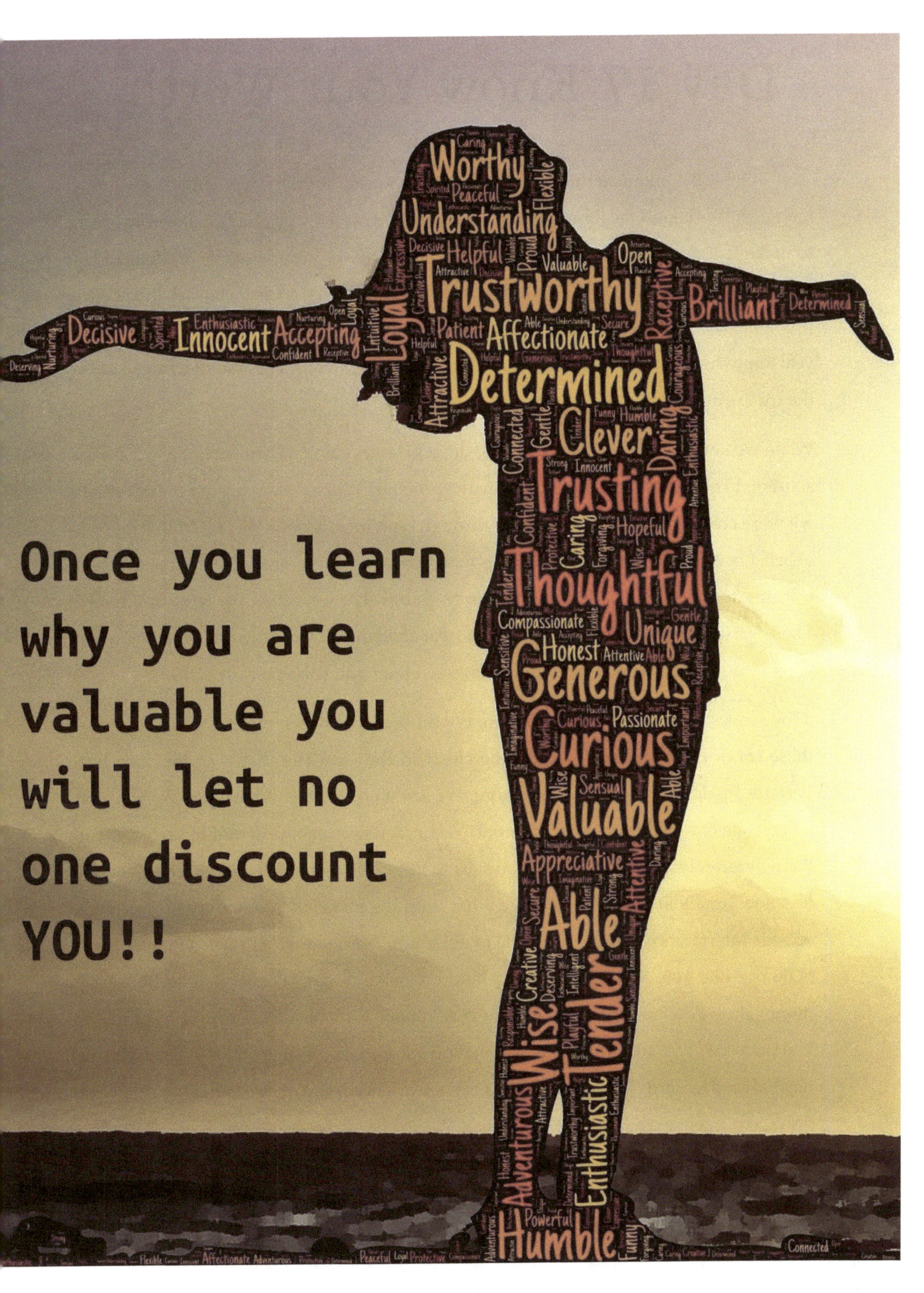

Day 17 Know Your Worth

Only the manufacturer of a thing can speak to the true value of it. The manufacturer knows the time, the tools, the resources, and the products that were needed to make it. To create something, the manufacturer knows what is inside and outside of what they created. The creator created it with a purpose. The creator created it to solve a problem. That's called purpose. I heard Dr. Myles Monroe say in a video created many years ago the definition of purpose is "God's original intent." The manufacturer knows the true value of it because he made it.

When we know what we were created to do, it gives us value. When we know we are the solution to a problem, we can stop being the problem. When we are unsure of the reason, we were created it is easy for us to go through searching for our WHY. On this journey of Self-Love, learning your value and knowing your worth is going to be the key to others learning to value you. Things that we love, things that we value, we treat differently. There is a difference between the way you treat an item you pay little for and an item that you pay a lot for. You will treat things based on their value to you.

I love shoes. I love shoes a lot and there is a difference between my everyday shoes and those shoes I keep tucked away in the closet in the shoe bag that is in the shoe box. Because I paid more, I value them more. We are no different!! Whenever you love and value someone you treat them different. You reverence them differently; you speak to them differently. Now is time that you start to Value who you are with that same energy. It is now time that you start to Value what is on the inside of you and no longer allow outside interference or outside people to determine your value. You are valuable. There is no one like you. You are a one-of-a-kind exclusive design. Things that are rare have more value. You are one of a kind; that is as rare as it comes. Being rare is what makes you priceless. You are gifted with gifts that no one else has. You are talented and you are needed on this Earth. You are here because you are needed. You are valuable.

Take some time and think about the way you treat you. Why is it so important for you to evaluate the way you treat you? It is because we teach others how to treat us by how we treat ourselves. The way others treat us is a direct reflection of how we treat ourselves. We teach people how to value us by how they see us value us. We are always teaching people how to treat us and how to value us by the way you love you. Others will love and value you by what they see you do to you. When you learn your true value; you will no longer accept those in your space who treat you less than your value. Do not let others discount you. Begin to set boundaries for what is acceptable and what is not. Unaddressed misuse leads to abuse. Be clear and concise about those boundaries and stand on them.

The consumer never determines the worth of the item. The Manufacturer provides a Suggested Retail Price. This is the least the item should be sold for based upon the value from the one who made it. The creator of the thing can only determine the value of a thing. Psalm 139:14 says, "you are fearfully and wondrously made." Stop discounting yourself!!! You do not have to change who you are to get people to like you. Embrace You. You are dope and do not dull your dopeness for nobody. You do not have to lessen your light to make someone else feel good about themselves. People say to me all the time that I'm extra, but the issue really isn't that I'm extra it's that they are uncomfortable because they are basic. We were created in the likeness of God so that means we are great because He is great. We are creators because he is a creator. We have been gifted with the ability to produce. So, surround yourself with people who celebrate you and not just tolerate you. Remember you are wondrously made. Do not try to put right pieces in wrong places; there are those who love you, value you, care for you and value being your presence.

When we value ourselves, we treat ourselves differently and do not allow others to devalue us. People can only do to us what we allow them to do. Getting to know who you are and getting to know your value will require you changing your mindset about God and you.

I remember sitting in the library at Valdosta State University and I started making a checklist of "who am I" and what I bring to the table. Making this list revealed to me my true value. I did not think about what I was not, I did not think about what I could not do. I did not consider my size, education, or financial status. I thought about what Mechelle has to offer with her many gifts, abilities, and talents. After having that internal conversation about my value with myself, my life changed. I started handling me differently. I started valuing and celebrating who I am. I started to have confidence in my skills, my gifts, and my abilities like never before. When I saw me differently others started too as well. Disrespect was no longer acceptable and when it happened it did not go unaddressed. Remember, unaddressed misuse leads to abuse. Minimizing myself so others could feel comfortable stopped. I was no longer devaluing myself to fit in or be liked. I learned who Mechelle really was and loved me unconditionally. I started valuing me and required others to value me. It was only when I discovered how much God loved me and he had a reason for creating me. I was masterfully created on purpose for a purpose. Certain manufacturers like Louis Vuitton, Tiffany & Co and Chanel never have a sale on their product because they don't discount their product because they know the value of it. Because they have a base of customers who value the product and the name so much that they will purchase it at full price. You are valuable and should never be discounted. Those who see your worth will pay full price.

Accept yourself as a work in progress the continue

to build yourself into the person you're dreaming to be;

the person you have all the potential to be.

accept your flaws, accept your truths. accept your past.

and make light of them. No one can tear you down if

you make peace with who you are and where you've

been. ~ Reyna Biddy

Self-Love Exercise: Below are 2 price tags. If you could place a monetary value to yourself, what would it be? Write your value on one side of the price tag and on the other write the reasons you believe you are valued at the dollar amount. This may take some time for you to do and that is okay. Walk away and come back and review it again until you can complete this exercise. If you don't know what makes you valuable, you will always discount yourself. If you want to really know your worth and your purpose consult God, your creator because He knows. When we realize that our value is on display daily in the way we walk, talk, and act, we become more aware of how we handle ourselves, our situations, and circumstances. When you realize you are the answer you stop being the problem. Don't discount you because you are worth every penny.

Self-Love Journal Exercise: Take some time to journal about a recent situation when you did not act or react according to the price on your price tag. Think about what happened and why it happened the way it did. Also, journal about how you can do things differently the next time so that you can show your value. When you display your value then others will value you. You are not responsible for what others do but you are responsible for how you react. The way you respond will either show your true value or discount your value the choice is yours.

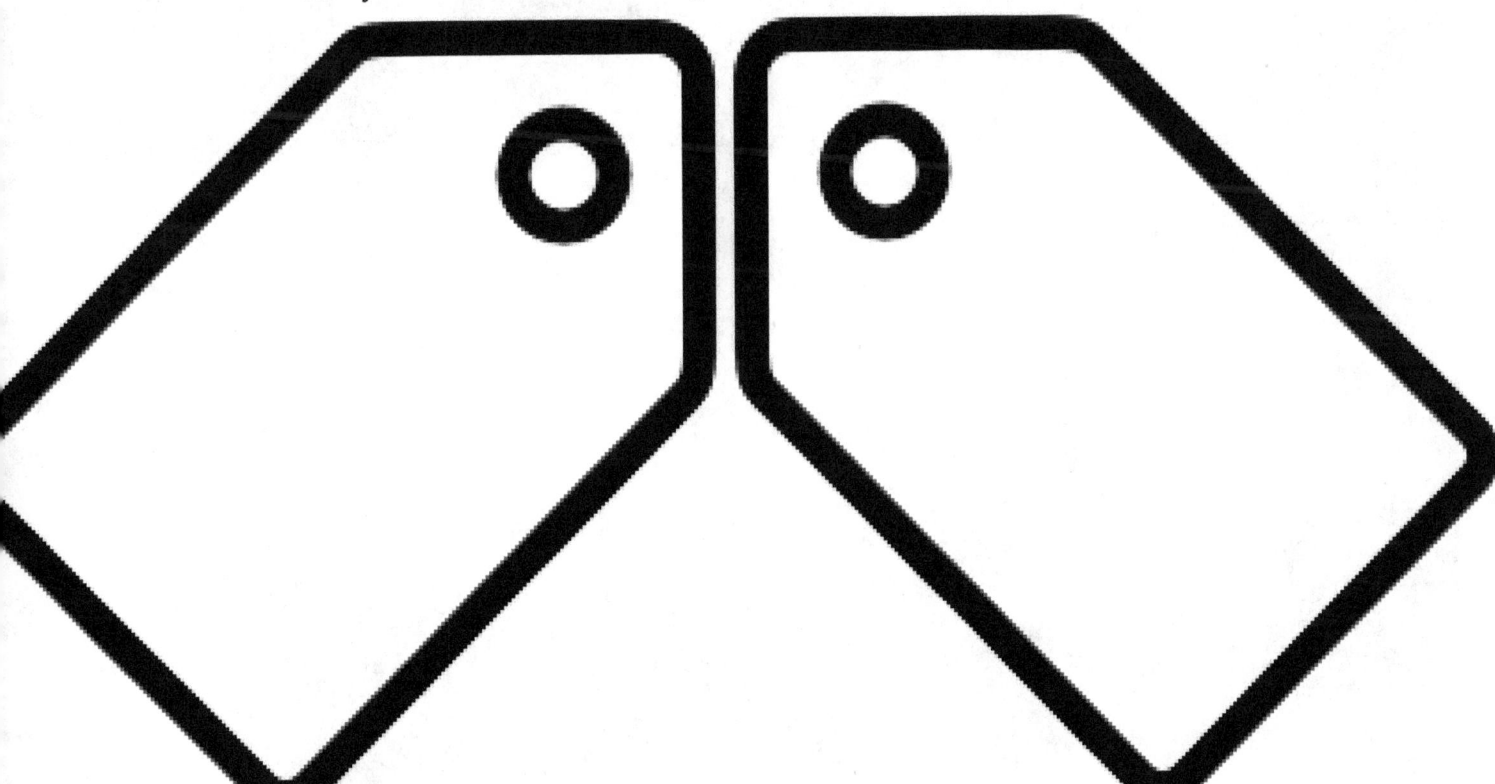

PURSUE

PURPOSE

Day 18 Find Your Purpose

Everything created was created with a gift inside of it. Everything that was naturally created was created with the ability to reproduce of its own kind. Everything that was created can self-sustain in the right environment without outside interference. That is the way God created everything on the Earth. When we look at the gift of the seed it is the tree inside of it. We look at the tree and see the gift of the tree is the ability to bear fruit. When we look at the fruit the gift of the fruit is the substance is it provides, and the seed inside the fruit gives it the ability to create others of its kind.

Today, we look on the outside to find our purpose when our purpose lies within. Inside of this Earthen vessel is treasures, gifts, and the ability to recreate of its same kind both physically and spiritually. Your true purpose isn't found in anything outside of you. Your purpose has been placed inside you. You do not have to look at others to find out your purpose. You will never find your true purpose looking on the outside of you. Your purpose is connected to your gifts, your purpose is connected to your ability to make others of your kind. Whatever that gift is connected to is what you are supposed to leave in this earth. Gifts are given to be given away. A seed never says I am going to keep the tree inside me because it is my gift, but it gives the gift of the tree. The tree never says I am going to keep my fruit because it is my fruit, but it gives it away. The same with you and I our gifts don't just benefit others, but it also benefits us. We are put here on this Earth to give our gifts away.

No one takes a gift, wraps it, and keeps it. The gift does not become a gift until you give it away. If you hold on to it, it is not a gift. Gifting does not happen until you do the process of giving it away. The same with your purpose, your purpose lies down within you. It is not hiding but it does have to be discovered. It does not have to be found or located; it must be tapped into. Because it is on the inside of you, your gift and your purpose cannot be taught. You are the only one who can make it happen. Remember it is God's original intent for creating you.

Your purpose here on this earth is to recreate others like you physically and spiritually. If you are not giving of your gift, then you have not tapped into your purpose. Gifts are on the inside of you and should not be compared to the gifts of anyone else. There can be one hundred fruits on a tree, but no two fruits are identical. Same as with your gift, there may be hundreds of people with the same gift that you have, but no one can fulfill your purpose but you because that was the reason you were created. Do not rob the earth of YOU.

We look on the outside to find our purpose when our purpose lies inside of YOU. We have this gift in earthen treasures. You are so perfect; flaws and all. Learn to love all of you the way the master creator does. You will never find your true purpose looking on the outside of you. Look within and identify your gifts, your purpose is connected to your ability, to make others of your kind. Whatever that gift is connected to, is what you are supposed to leave in this Earth. Gifts are given to be given away.

The number of gifts does not determine the amount of impact. Whether you have one, three, five or fourteen gifts it does not matter. It is the usage of those gifts that determine your greatness and success. Do not measure or compare your gift to that of someone else. Do not measure or compare the number of gifts you have to someone else because if you take your one gift and use it you are just as impactful as someone who has many gifts, but they don't operate in the spirit of excellence. Excellence isn't perfect but it is the best you can do with what you have. That's all God wants is that you give your very best. You are unique and there is no one like you. You are created to solve a problem in the earth so find that problem and solve it. It is not hard to find, it is down on the inside of you and is connected to the gift. Search your soul and find out the things that you like to do and the things that you do well. It could be the problem that you find yourself always solving. According to Webster's definition a gift, is the inherited ability to do something. So, whatever that inherent ability to do, it is your gift. The ability to do something very well, better than others is what is connected to your purpose. You use your natural gifts and God will add the super for you to operate in the Supernatural. It is a buried treasure, buried down on the inside of you and you only find it by searching on the inside of you. Search your heart, your mind, your soul, your gift, and talent find that purpose and pursue it. You were created on purpose for a purpose. You were not a mistake. You were put on earth for a specific reason. You are someone's answer, and they are awaiting you to discover your purpose. Pursue Purpose.

Self-Love Exercise: Take some time and identify what your gifts are? Gift meaning "a notable capacity, talent, or endowment" according to Merriam Webster definition. By identifying your gifts, they will point you to your purpose.

1.

2.

3.

4.

5.

Think about the things you can do, and you get so much fulfillment that you will do it for free. That is what you are supposed to be doing!!!! List at least three

1.

2.

3.

Self-Love Journal Exercise:

If finances were not an issue in your life, what would you be doing? If you could be anything in the world what would that be? Journal about what you would do and pursue them.

Past   Present

Don't let your past disrupt your present.

Day 19 Live Now in the Present

For years I was a victim of what I call Stolen Moments. What I mean by Stolen Moments is you are here, but you cannot embrace here because you are stuck in your past. You cannot embrace what is happening right now because of what happened years ago. It is still holding onto you and is dictating how you move and live today. You are unable to make current decisions because of bad past decisions. We often feel that way because we do not know the magic of "dance in the moment." Something happens that triggers a past trauma and your mind is hijacked and mentally you are transported back to the place of the trauma. Old hurts can be triggered and awakened; they will hold onto you. We are not taught to be in this current moment or dancing in the moment even when you are triggered. Your current moment is an important moment because tomorrow it will be your past. Where you are right now, your current moment is the key to your healing, happiness, and success. Not to say that what has happened to you cannot help you through what is going on in your life right now, but if it is still causing you hurt, you have some work to do.

If what you are currently going through is being hindered by the trauma of your past there is still some work to do. Love yourself enough to work to be free from your past, this way you can move forward into your future without being caught in stolen moments of your past. Think about it this way, you made it through whatever trauma happened in your life. It did not kill you. You survived it, so why let the memory of the situation kill you. The actual event itself did not kill you. It is time to take control of your right now and dance in it no matter what it looks like. You cannot control what has happened, but you can control what will happen. Embrace your now!! Your every moment dance in it!! It will not always be good, but every day you are alive it is a chance to change the narrative. You can't rewrite the beginning of your story, but you can decide what the end will look like. Write your ending.

I know you are thinking Coach Mechelle, that sounds good and all but is it really something that can be done? My answer is absolutely!! You can live in the right now. You can dance in every moment. Right now, like right now you can feel, live, and embrace you. To get from point A to point B using the GPS it asks to access your current location. That is how you start to live now and not in the past by identifying your current location. You cannot tell the GPS where you want to go without telling it where you are right now. The GPS has to measure the distance from where you are to where you are going. What you don't measure you can't manage. In this journey of self-love, you must learn to give yourself permission to embrace you right where you are. No longer live your life based on the past but be free to walk in your present. Regardless of the situation and circumstances you can dance in it. You can be free; you must take the steps to get to that place. Recognizing where you are and understanding how you got there will help you to not repeat your past mistakes. Acknowledging what you can do differently and making the necessary adjustment is vital to not allowing your past to steal the moments of your present.

Self-Love Exercise: Identify where you are in your life right now if you are not in love with yourself say aloud, "I am not in love with me or I have not been loving me like I should." Think about the trauma of your past that always seems to come up and cause havoc in your right now. There may be some people, areas, or situations you may have to take your power back from; if it has control it has the power. If you can't do this alone, seek help. Learn to ask for help and accept it when it comes. Even if the help you need is learning to be present in your right now. Dance In It!!

The Wheel of Life.

Take time to complete the wheel of life and be honest with yourself about where you currently are. Again, what you don't measure you can't manage. Remember identifying where you are right now is important to you moving forward in your journey. This will help you identify the areas in your life where you are doing amazing and your areas of opportunity.

HOW TO COMPLETE THE WHEEL OF LIFE:

1. Review the 8 Wheel Categories - think briefly what a satisfying life might look like for you in each area.

2. Next, draw a line across each segment that represents your satisfaction score for each area.

- Imagine the center of the wheel is 0 and the outer edge is 10
- Choose a value between 1 (very dissatisfied) and 10 (fully satisfied)
- Now draw a line and write the score alongside (see example above)

IMPORTANT: Use the FIRST number (score) that pops into your head, not the number you think it *should* be!

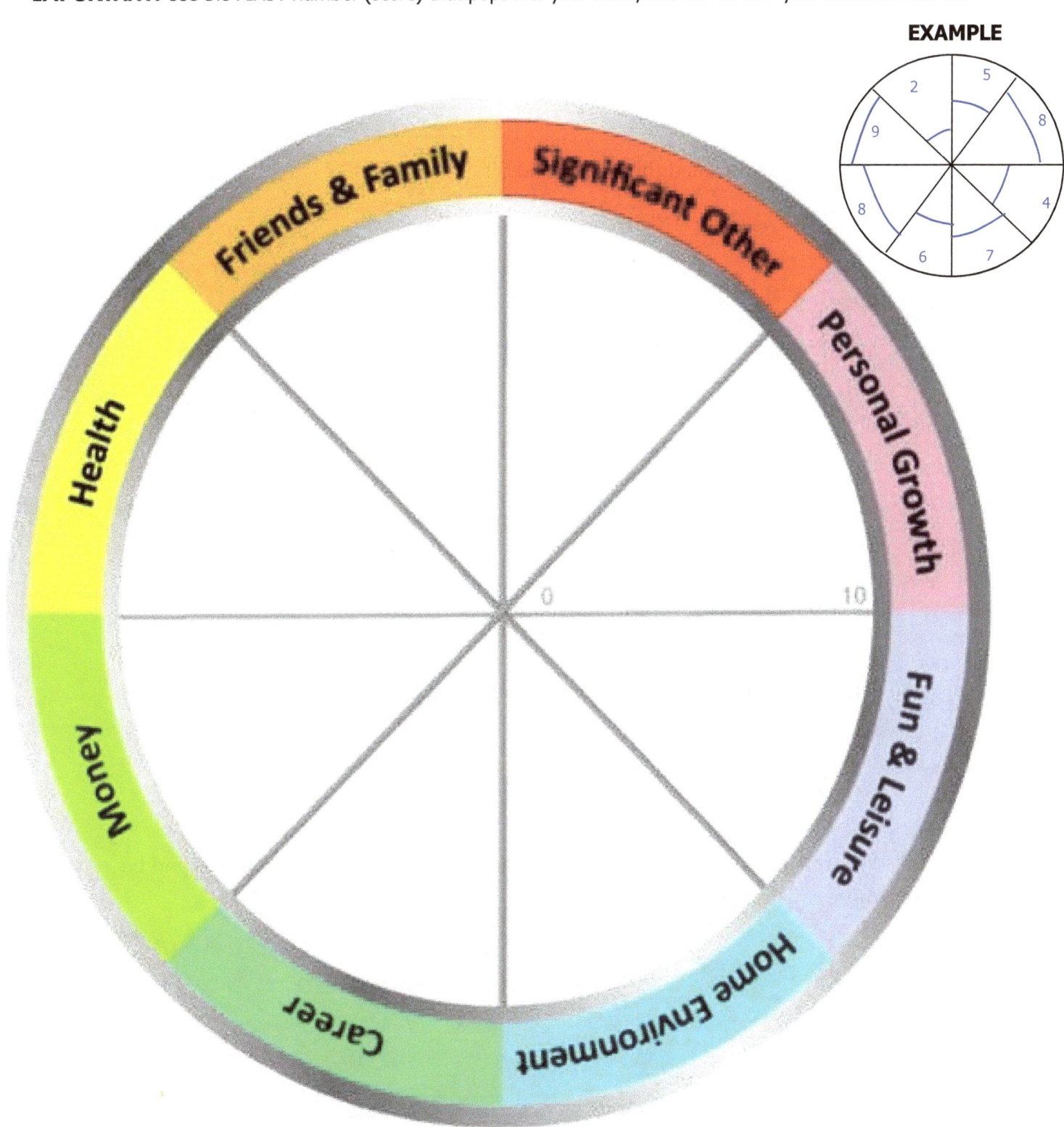

Self-Love Journal Exercise: Answer the following 7 questions about the results of your Wheel of Life. If you find yourself triggered by your answers take some time to journal.

1. How do you feel about your life after reviewing the results of your Wheel of Life?

2. Are you surprised?

3. Which area you rated the lowest and why?

4. Which are you most satisfied and why?

5. Which of these categories would you most like to improve?

6. How could you make space for these changes in your life?

7. What help and support might you need from others to make changes and be more satisfied with your life?

Day 20 No One Compares to You

There is an acronym that has become popular in our time, and it is used to describe someone who has done something greater than those who have come before them and greater than those who may come after them. People like Michael Jackson, Michael Jordan, Tiger Woods, Barack Obama, Michelle Obama, and Oprah. People of this caliber have been referred to as the G.O.A.T. Meaning they are the "Greatest of All Times." The above-named people are all G.O.A.T.S. They are all known as the greatest of all times in each of their own right. Not many can be compared to them. Their skills, gifts and talents are second to none.

There has not been anyone before you or anyone after you who can be compared to you. You are a G.O.A.T. You are the greatest of all time. You might say how can you say that. I can say it with blessed assurance because there will never be another like you. No one before, no one after you. You are the only you. No one can be a better you than you. You are the best you. There is no comparison to who you are. **2 Corinthians 10:12** "For we dare not make ourselves of the number or compare ourselves with some that commend themselves: but they measuring themselves by themselves, and comparing themselves among themselves, are not wise." (AKJV) We are unwise when we are comparing ourselves to others. There is no one who measures up to you. Who you are and your success cannot be compared or measured to the success of others because there is no one like you.

"Don't compare yourself to others. You have no idea what their journey is all about." ~ Dawn Abraham

The old cliché' says, "you can't compare apples to oranges." When it comes to comparing you to someone like you or even someone unlike you there is no comparison. Take twins for instance, even though they may share some identical, same womb, and same birthday they are still different. Even twins cannot be compared. there is absolutely no one on this earth who can compare to you. There is no one who can be the standard for you because we are all uniquely created. You are the greatest you of all time.

"Comparison is the thief of joy." ~ Theodore Roosevelt.

Johnathan McReynolds sings a song titled "Comparisons Kill" and they do. Whenever you try to compare your life to someone else's life, you overlook how amazingly gifted you are. Comparing your gift to someone else's gift, may cause you to feel like you are insignificant. Comparison will rob you of your joy. It will steal from you the gleam in your eye. Although identical twins share some features and DNA, they are still different. If twins are no comparison for each other then there is absolutely no one on this earth who can be compared to you. I say to you that you are the greatest you of all time. No one can do you like you. No one can be like you. So, embrace you and be confident in you knowing that when you walk in the building no one can do you like you do. When you walk in the room greatness enters the room. Never be afraid to be authentically you. Remember it's you that the world needs and not a watered-down version of someone you are pretending to be.

"A flower does not think of competing to the flower next to it. It just blooms." ~ Zen Shin

One of my favorite parts of the song Comparison Kills says "The grass was fine until it looks greener on the other side. Now you believing that you fell behind. Why try to match what should be one of a kind. You are one of a kind" I love this part of the song because we are often in a good space until we start to look and compare ourselves to the liking of someone else. You are great just as you are. Be okay in the skin you are in because no one can compare to you.

Self-Love Exercise: For the next 3 days look in the mirror and tell yourself in "THERE IS NO ONE AS GREAT AS YOU."

The next time you walk in a room, and you are feeling intimidated by who is in the room. Close your eyes and envision yourself getting taller. Walk in the room tall and proud because "THERE IS NO ONE AS GREAT AS YOU."

Self-Love Journal: After telling yourself "THERE IS NO ONE AS GREAT AS YOU" Journal how it made you feel. You should tell yourself this daily. This is just the start of you knowing that you are great.

Bonus Exercise: Below are 5 Affirmation from the scriptures. Read these often until you began to see you like God sees you.

1. I am valuable (1 Peter 1:18-19)

2. I am remarkably made (Psalm 139:14, Genesis 1:27)

3. I am forgiven (1 John 1:9, Ephesians 1:7, Colossians 3:13)

4. I am enough (2 Peter 1:3, 2 Corinthian 3:5, Colossians 2:10)

5. I am accepted (Romans 15:7, Ephesians 1:3-6, Colossians 1:21-22)

Day 21 Make Time for You

      We take time for so many things, so many people, and so much stuff. We plan, we set aside, and we coordinate time to spend with others. The one person that gets neglected is you. We find ourselves burned out and frustrated and ready to give up because we do not take time for ourselves, time to reset, recharge, and unwind. We continue to go day after day without taking time to gather our thoughts and just be in a quiet moment with ourselves. We may think that with all we do, there is no time for us to take a day to ourselves you must schedule time in your day for you. To be available for yourself and be present in your feeling. You must plan time to spend with yourself, you will discover that there is a lot about you that you are unaware of because you have never taken the time to get to know you.

In this journey to self-love, self-awareness is key. You must take time to discover who you are and get to know yourself. Whenever we are courting or dating someone, we take time to find out what they like and their dislikes, their beliefs and what they like to do. Because we want to know them for who they are, but I want to pose this question to you. Who are you? Have you taken the time to find out Who You Are? Have you taken to the time to find out what you have down on the inside of you? Most of us don't have a clue. In order to learn to love you and identify more ways to connect to you and love more on you that requires you spending time with yourself. You have to be intentional about the relationship you have with you.

I remember a time in my life when I did not like the person I had become. I did not want to spend time with that person because of the things I allowed to take place in my life. Because of the abuse and misuse, I allowed. I discovered I was no longer the victim of my hurt but a participant. I did not like looking at myself in the mirror because I did not know who I was anymore. I had to confront the hurt and trauma in my life. The dysfunction, the abuse, and the disappointment in order for me to love me again, but once I accepted the fact that I had taken part in allowing my abuser to abuse me, I could then start on my road to recovery. I realized I helped him hurt me. I started doing the work on me and in me. I got focused on me and owned my story. Because I took ownership in the place I was in my life and my discovery of learning to love myself, I started spending more time with me and less time with others. Dr. Myles Monroe has a message titled "The Five Keys to Success" and the first key to success is learning "who am I?" I want to pose this question to you again, Who are you?

Before you answer the question do not think about who you are connected to, do not think about the fact that you are parent or wife, a partner, the company you work for, your religious affiliation, and do not think about being a child because none of those things are who you are. Right now, ask yourself "who am I?" Learning to love yourself will begin with you learning who you are and spending time getting to know who you really are.

I started with simply taking 7 minutes in the morning to myself. Before my feet hit the floor, I take time for me. I use this time to meditate pray and center myself. This helps me to focus on my day and it gets me grounded. I used to get up at 5:30am. I used to have a 5:30am alarm and then I have a 5:37am alarm. This is me being intentional about the time I spend with me. Making myself a priority

It does not seem like a lot of time, but it is not about the quantity but the quality. Research states how you spend the first 20 minutes of your day will determine the outcome of your day. This is a great start.

Self-Love Exercise: I want to challenge you to start spending time with you starting tomorrow. Schedule at least 7 minutes of me time. Make this a nonnegotiable in your day. Commit yourself to doing this for the next 21 days. Be protective over this time keeping this time sacred.

Self-Love Journal Exercise: Write an apology letter to yourself for not taking time for yourself. Recommit yourself to loving on yourself and be intentional about you. **Bonus Exercise:** Take time to schedule your ME time for the next 21 days on the daily planner provided.

My weekly time with me

Be intentional and schedule your ME time for the next 21 days

Monday	Tuesday

Wednesday	Thursday

Friday	Saturday

Sunday	Notes:

My weekly time with me

> Be intentional and schedule your ME time for the next 21 days

Monday	Tuesday
Wednesday	Thursday
Friday	Saturday
Sunday	**Notes:**

My weekly time with me

Be intentional and schedule your ME time for the next 21 days

Monday	Tuesday
Wednesday	Thursday
Friday	Saturday
Sunday	Notes:

Self-Love Journal

Self-Love Journal

Self-Love Journal

Self-Love Journal

Self-Love Journal

Self-Love Journal

Self-Love Journal

Self-Love Journal

Self-Love Journal

Self-Love Journal

Self-Love Journal

Self-Love Journal

Self-Love Journal

Self-Love Journal

Self-Love Journal

Self-Love Journal

Self-Love Journal

Self-Love Journal

Self-Love Journal

Self-Love Journal

Self-Love Journal

Self-Love Journal

Self-Love Journal

Self-Love Journal

Embrace You Coaching
PRESENTS

Master Life Coach Mechelle Canady

LIFE COACH

**LIFE COACH CERTIFICATION
BUSINESS COACHING
SPIRITUAL COACHING
STRATEGY COACHING
CLARITY COACHING
EXECUTIVE COACHING**

If you are interested in becoming a Certified Life Coach email us at info@embrace4you.com

 @coachmechellecanady

 WWW.EMBRACE4YOU.COM

 @mrsgetu2gether

 @mrsgetu2gether